Disclaimer:
The information presented in this book represents the views of the publisher as of the date of publication. The publisher reserves the rights to alter update their opinions based on new conditions. This report is for informational purposes only. The author and the publisher do not accept any responsibilities for any liabilities resulting from the use of this information. While every attempt has been made to verify the information provided here, the author and the publisher cannot assume any responsibility for errors, inaccuracies or omissions. Any similarities with people or facts are unintentional

Table of contents

Introduction 5
    Persian Rice: Rice Like You Have Never Had Before 6

Chapter 1 9
The Art of Cooking Rice 9
Chapter 2 13
Rice with Meats (Chicken, Beef and Lamb) 13
    KOOFTEH BERENJI 18
    ADAS POLOW 21
    BAGHALI POLOW WITH CHICKEN 23
    SHIRAZI POLOW 25

Chapter 3 27
    SABZEH POLOW BA MAHI

.... 31

Chapter 4 34
    CHESHM BOLBOLI POLOW 35
    LUBIA POLOW.. 38
    ZERESHK POLOW... 41
    SHIRIN POLOW... 44
    KALAM POLOW.. 47
    DAMI BAGHALI.. 50
    DOLMEH Y KALAM.. 52
    MORASAH POLOW... 54
    TAHDIG SIBZAMINI.. 57
    ESTAMBOLI POLOW 59
    BAGHALI POLOW... 63
    ALBALOO POLOW.. 65

Chapter 5 68
    More Facts about Saffron..................................... 70
    The Saffron Plant.. 71

Chapter 6 73

4

Introduction

Rice may not be a staple in all cuisines, but in Asian, and especially in Persian Cooking, it plays a very important role in the meal planning. Prepared to be paired with various dishes (vegetables, seafood and meats), rice meals are planned to fill up meals and raise the dining experience by a notch or two. More so, rice dishes provide a good source of carbohydrates for energy.

Ordinarily, rice is boiled. Other rice dishes are merely seasoned with some flavor, but in the case of Persian cooking, a true exploration will be experienced because the preparation of Persian Rice requires true devotion. Chefs are expected to laboriously boil, sauté, layer and bake the rice and, with the myriad of ingredients available to be utilized, the variety is one you can eagerly anticipate.

Persian Rice: Rice Like You Have Never Had Before

Of the many ancient cuisines, Persian cuisine is one with roots that date back to the ancient era of the world. With its age, it has been present long enough to influence many other cuisines: Roman, Asian, Mediterranean and Greek. The profile of the food is different from area to area, so it is normal for you to find cookbooks showcasing the different regions and tastes of Ancient Iran that have been preserved, perfected and enhanced for a thousand of years.

The characteristic thing about Iranian cooking is its antiquity and culture. Traditionally, wives and mothers manned the spectacular kitchens of fine palaces and humble homes. The dominance of women in Iranian cooking persists today with many of the renowned

chefs still being female.

Much thought is given to every Iranian meal, especially those held at home. When Iranians dine, tables are adorned with a combination of hot and cold meals. Diners are served with a collection of poultry, animal fat, wheat, fresh fruits and vegetables, beef, dairy products, fish and rice. Rice, the perfect meal filler, and a good source of carbohydrates and energy, is one dish that you cannot ignore with every Persian meal. It is a major ingredient in many Persian dishes, being cooked using different types of rice grains, and incorporating different kinds of flavors.

Chapter 1
The Art of Cooking Rice

Ancient Persia was founded in 549 BCE by Cyrus the Great. In the years following its discovery, it dominated the ancient world for the length of two hundred years. It enjoyed dominion to the east in Asia and to the west in Egypt; their food adapted to the area's culinary culture as the nomad kings took their travels from one capital to another – enjoying winters in Babylon for their wine, autumn in Persepolis where wild fruits and vegetables were abundant, and spring in Ecbatana for the meats, herbs and dairy products.

Persian dishes are known for their creative mix of various spices, much of them borrowed from the Indian cuisine. It could be said, therefore, that the similarities between Turkish and Persian dishes often confuse the palette into properly identifying their true origins. One thing you have to know is that Persian cooking focuses on very characteristic ingredients. Like in most cultures, you get to identify and characterize the cuisine through the use of key ingredients. In the case of Persian cooking, basil, pomegranate, pea, cumin, sesame, olive, saffron, coriander, cloves, walnut, pistachio and mint are part of the list of its signature ingredients.

A great part of Persian cooking is the preparation of rice dishes, showcasing many of the signature ingredients. The variety of flavors developed through the combination of grains, nuts, meats, vegetables and spices (and not forgetting the sprinkling of saffron to top each dish!) give it a true Persian touch.

When rice is cooked, it is steamed to perfection to bring out all its fragrance and flavor. From pieces of grains they are transformed to plain rice and eaten with stew or meat. They may also be steamed along with other ingredients, such as meat, vegetables, sour cherries, herbs and pulses, to name a few, that does not only give it a unique taste, but also enhances its color and texture. Given that Persian cooking dates back to the ancient empires, today's dishes are still very reminiscent of how they were when served to kings, queens and other great leaders of empires. Today's dishes still exhibit delicate detail with garnishes such as saffron, orange peel, barberries, almonds and pistachios.

In preparing Persian Rice Dishes, there are some terms that one needs to be familiar with. You will find that this book will help to equip you appropriately, so that you can enjoy a smooth Persian cooking journey:

- Chelow: This type of cooking goes through two stages: soaking and parboiling before the water is drained and the rice is rinsed. The white rice is sautéed in butter and steamed with a small amount of water. In the end, what you enjoy is rice that is very light and fluffy with separate grains. The chelow method sometimes also results in "tahdig", a golden rice crust at the bottom of the pot.
- Kateh: This kind of rice cooking results in very characteristic, sticky rice. This method of preparation begins with traditional boiling, but at a reduced heat. Basically, it follows the most traditional method of cooking rice, where the grains are allowed to absorb most of the water.
- Polow: Here, rice is cooked in a broth, resulting in separate rice grains. In this cooking method, the rice is cooked

conventionally. Upon reaching its half-cooked stage, it is strained carefully before having the broth added for brewing. In essence, it is prepared similarly to Chelow, but after draining and brewing the rice, other ingredients are added to be cooked with the rice. To avoid confusion, remember this – Chelow: plain rice; Polow: Chelow rice with vegetables, herbs, and/or meat.

- Dami: This method is similar to Kateh, but instead of following the traditional method, the heat is reduced before boiling point is reached. In addition, a towel is placed between the lid and the pot so that the steam is kept from escaping. As a result, you get the full effect of simmering, such that the grains stick together and appear moist.
- Biryani and Tajine: These types of rice preparation follow a slow cooking method that is often combined with meat and vegetables.

Given all that, you have to really understand one important thing about Persian Rice Cooking – it is more an art than anything else. In most places, rice is merely placed in a pot and boiled until soft, but that is not how the Persian cuisine works. When rice is cooked and prepared for a Persian meal, the chef devotes a great deal of time and effort to ensure that something magnificent will be created.

Chapter 2

Rice with Meats (Chicken, Beef and Lamb)

Meats play a big role in Persian cuisine, especially chicken, beef and lamb. Grilled and skewered meats are very popular, and they also find their way into rice dishes. Depending on the amount of meat you add, and when it is added, your dish will either become your entire meal, or simply have its flavors and character transformed.

MORGH POLOW

Preparation time: 2-3 hours
Cooking Time:
Serves: 4

Ingredients

4 chicken thighs
3 cups basmati or long-grain rice
1½ cups zereshk (barberry)
½ cup and 2 tablespoons water, divided
1 medium-sized onion, chopped
2 cloves garlic, crushed
6 tablespoons brewed saffron, divided*
2-3 tablespoons unsalted butter
2-3 tablespoons canola oil
2 tablespoons and ¼ teaspoon salt, divided
1 tablespoon sugar
½ teaspoon turmeric powder
¼ teaspoon ground black pepper

Instructions

1. Wash the rice twice. Soak the rice with 1 tablespoon of salt for 2-3 hours. Drain the water.
2. Half fill a large pan with water and heat over a medium-flame until boiling.
3. Add the drained rice and another tablespoon of salt. Cook for 10 minutes, or until the rice is slightly soft. While cooking, gently scoop the rice from the bottom of the pot and fold it into the surface. Repeat this several times. Remove from the heat.
4. Carefully drain the rice and rinse it with cold water to stop the cooking process. Set aside.
5. Evenly place the onion and garlic on the bottom of a pot, and dust with ¼ teaspoon of turmeric powder.
6. Meanwhile, season the chicken with salt and pepper on both sides. Layer the chicken on top of the onions and garlic. Evenly sprinkle with the remaining turmeric powder.
7. Add ½ cup of water and cook, covered, over a medium flame for 30 minutes. Once cooked debone and coarsely shred the chicken. Set the stock and chicken aside.
8. Soak, wash, and rinse the zereshk with water a couple of times. Soak the zereshk in enough water for a few minutes to properly clean them. For the last time, rinse and drain the zereshk.
9. In a medium sauce pan, melt 2 tablespoons of butter. Add the zereshk and sugar. Mix well and add 2 tablespoons of brewed saffron. Stir a little and remove from the heat. Reserve ¼ cup of prepared zereshk.
10. In a non-stick pot add 2-3 tablespoons of canola oil, 2 tablespoons of water and 2 tablespoons of the brewed saffron.
11. Stir in 2-3 spatulas of the prepared rice and mix until the rice

is evenly coated with a yellow/orange color. Pat the rice down evenly in the pot.
12. Scoop another spatula of prepared rice on top of the yellow/orange rice. Add ⅓ of the prepared zereshk. Gently incorporate the zereshk into the prepared rice.
13. Layer with ⅓ of cooked chicken. Repeat layering with prepared rice, zereshk, and chicken, and finish with prepared rice.
14. Using the handle of your spatula, create a few holes on the rice. Cover and cook over a high flame for 10 minutes.
15. Meanwhile, strain the chicken broth, removing the garlic and onions. Mix this broth with the remaining 2 tablespoons of brewed saffron, and pour it over the rice.
16. Finally, seal the pot by wrapping the lid with a towel. Reduce heat to low and cook for about an hour.
17.

*prepared by steeping a pinch of saffron thread with 6 tablespoons of hot water for 2 hours.

Morgh Polow is also known as Persian Rice and Chicken, or simply as "Chicken Rice". While it is practically the same recipe as Zereshk Polow with Chicken, the main difference is that in Morgh Polow the chicken is steamed with the rice, infusing it with its flavor and essence. Zereshk Polow only features the chicken as a garnishing agent.

KOOFTEH BERENJI

Preparation time: 1½ to 2 hours
Cooking Time:
Serves: 6

Ingredients

1lb ground beef or lamb
3 cups water
2 cups mixed herbs (spring onion ends, parsley, common dill, sweet fennel, mint, tarragon), finely chopped and loosely packed
1 cup chickpea flour
1 cup zereshk (barberries)
1 cup walnuts

½ cup basmati or long grain rice
½ cup split peas
½ cup cooking oil
3 large eggs
3 medium-sized onions, sliced
1½ teaspoons turmeric powder
Salt and ground black pepper

Instructions

1. Cook the rice in salted water until it is soft. Carefully drain the water.
2. Boil the split peas, and cook until soft. Drain the water.
3. In a large bowl, mix the cooked rice, split peas, chickpea flour, eggs, herbs, ground beef or lamb, salt and pepper. Set aside.
4. Fry the onion slices until golden brown. Remove half of the fried onions and set them aside. Add 3 cups of water, some salt and pepper, and turmeric powder to the remaining fried onions in the pot, and boil over a medium-high heat.
5. Meanwhile, form large balls (orange size) with the prepared rice mixture. Insert bits of zereshk, walnuts and the reserved fried onions into the center of the balled mixture.
6. Place the balls in the turmeric water mixture, and cook for 50-60 minutes over a medium-low flame. Make sure that the koofteh are well soaked with water; if not, add more water and some seasonings. Cook them with the pot slightly open.

This recipe offers you a very unique way to enjoy rice. Koofteh Berenji is rice in a ball with surprises of herbs, meat, and all the other ingredients in the mixture. You are probably used to seeing rice loosely served, whether separate or sticky, but you may never have seen it in something as magnificent as this. You may sometimes find rice wrapped in lettuce or cabbage, or stuffed inside bell peppers, but not in a round ball mixture! This is a great way to enjoy rice at its fullest.

ADAS POLOW

Preparation Time: 4 to 5 hours
Cooking Time:
Serves: 4

Ingredients

1lb ground beef or lamb
2½ cups long-grain or basmati rice
2 cups lentils, washed
⅔ cup pitted dates, washed
⅔ cup raisins, washed
½ teaspoon saffron thread, steeped with ⅓ cup hot water
2 large-sized onions, thinly sliced
1 teaspoon salt
½ teaspoon turmeric powder
½ teaspoon ground black pepper
Cooking oil

Instructions

1. Soak the rice with water in a pot for 3-4 hours. Add a little bit of salt and cook over a medium flame for 10-15 minutes, or until soft. Drain the water and set the rice aside.
2. Using the same pot, boil 2-3 cups of water. Add the washed lentils and a pinch of salt. Cook over a medium heat for 15-20 minutes, or until tender. Drain and set aside.
3. In a large pan, heated over a medium flame, fry the onion slices in the oil until slightly golden. Add the ground beef or lamb, salt, turmeric powder and black pepper. Cook for a further 10 minutes.

4. Gradually add one cup of hot water into the onion mixture. Cook until the water has been mostly absorbed and evaporated.
5. In a non-stick pot, add ½ cup of water and some oil. Transfer half of the cooked rice into the pot. Add the meat, lentils, raisins and dates. Top with the remaining rice.
6. Cook the rice mixture over a low heat for about 20 minutes.
7. Pour the brewed saffron over the rice. Toss the mixture together before serving.

Adas Polow, also known as Lentil Rice, follows a method of delicate layering. By omitting the meat, this dish can be a perfect vegetarian meal - simple, and tasting great. In this particular dish, dates are added for flavor and texture, but you may opt to prepare the dish without them.

BAGHALI POLOW WITH CHICKEN

Preparation time: 1 to 1½ hours
Cooking Time:
Serves: 4

Ingredients

1lb chicken thighs
2 cups basmati or long-grain rice
2 cups fava beans
3 bunches dill, minced
1 tablespoon oil
1 teaspoon turmeric powder
½ teaspoon salt

Instructions

1. In a pot heated over a medium flame, add the chicken, water to cover the chicken, salt and turmeric powder. Let it simmer for about 30 minutes. Remove the chicken and set the broth aside.
2. Using the same pot, cook the fava beans with water until they are tender. Remove from the heat. Carefully peel off the skin of the fava beans and set them aside.
3. In another large pot, add the rice, chicken stock, dill and salt. Stir well and let it simmer until the water has evaporated.
4. In a separate pot, heat the oil and add the chicken. Carefully arrange the fava beans on top.
5. Cover the pot with a tea towel, put the lid on, and cook over low heat for about 20 minutes.

6. Combine everything before serving.

   Baghali Polo is usually a vegetarian rice dish that features beans and dill. For this particular recipe, however, chicken makes a useful appearance that contributes to the taste and texture of the dish. The addition of the chicken turns the simple rice side-dish into a complete meal.

SHIRAZI POLOW

Preparation time: 2 to 2½ hours
Cooking Time:
Serves: 4

Ingredients

3lb chicken breasts or thighs, skinless and boneless
3 cups basmati or long-grain rice
1 cup yogurt
1 cup and 1 tablespoon unsalted butter, divided
1 cup zereshk (barberries), washed, rinsed and drained
½ cup water
2 medium-sized eggplants, peeled and sliced
2 egg yolks
1 medium-sized onion, chopped
2 teaspoons brewed saffron*
1 teaspoon sugar
½ teaspoon salt
⅛ teaspoon ground black pepper
cooking oil

Instructions

1. Preheat the oven to 375°F.
2. In a large pan, sauté the chicken and onions until the chicken has turned lightly brown.
3. Add the water to the pan and cook the chicken for 30 minutes, or until fully cooked. Remove the chicken and set aside the broth.
4. Meanwhile, sauté the eggplants in the oil. Once cooked, remove from the heat and pat-dry with paper.
5. In a medium pan, mix together the sugar and 1 tablespoon of butter. Stir in the zereshk and cook over a low heat for 3 minutes. Set aside.
6. In a large bowl, whisk together the egg yolks, saffron and yogurt. Add the rice and gently mix.
7. In a greased 11" x 9" glass dish, add half of the rice mixture. Arrange the chicken pieces and fried eggplants over the rice, and top with the remaining rice.
8. Melt 1 cup of butter and mix it with the chicken stock. Pour the liquid over the rice before covering the entire dish with aluminum foil.
9. Bake for 1-2 hours, or until the crust has turned golden brown.
10. Serve inverted, and top with the prepared zereshk.

*prepared by steeping a pinch of saffron thread with 6 tablespoons of hot water for 2 hours.

It is not always common to have baked rice, but this recipe, though laboriously prepared, is an exceptional way to make crispy rice. Instead of cooking it traditionally on the stove, this dish is baked until crisp, proving every bite with just enough taste and texture.

Chapter 3

Rice with Seafood

Seafood is also an important ingredient in the Iranian cuisine. Like most rice dishes, the incorporation of fish, shrimps and crabmeat into the recipes makes the dining experience so much more exciting. Persian Rice Dishes are mostly vegetarian than anything else, but sometimes diners will demand more flavor, and when you are not so keen about meats, you can choose to find the extra flavor and texture from seafood.

MEIGOO POLOW

Preparation Time: 1 to 1½ hours
Cooking Time:
Serves: 4

Ingredients

1lb large shrimps
2½ cups basmati or long-grain rice
1½ cups parsley, coarsely chopped
⅔ cup butter
3-4 large eggs, hard-boiled

2 tablespoons tomato paste
1-2 tablespoons curry powder
1 tablespoon flour
cooking oil
salt and ground black pepper

Instructions

1. Wash the rice twice with water to clean it thoroughly. Drain.
2. Pour the rice into a non-stick pan. Mix it with 5 cups of water, 4 tablespoons of oil, and ½ teaspoon of salt.
3. Bring the water to a boil over a high flame until the level of the water reduces to just below the rice level.
4. Cover the pot, lower the flame to low, and cook for another half an hour.
5. Meanwhile, wash the shrimps. Transfer the shrimps to a pot of salted water and cook over a medium heat for 10 minutes, or until there is about ½ cup of water left. Set aside the shrimps and reserve the cooking liquid.
6. In a pan heated over a medium flame, make a roux by combining flour with butter, cooking for about 5 minutes.
7. Mix the tomato paste with the shrimp stock. Add this mixture, gradually, to the roux whilst constantly stirring.
8. Add salt, black pepper and curry powder. Mix until well combined. Cook for another 2-3 minutes. Remove from the heat.
9. Add the shrimps and mix well. Serve with the prepared rice, topping with sliced hard boiled eggs and parsley.

Meigoo Polow is also known as Persian Shrimp Rice. The preparation of this dish is very versatile. One can easily make it depending on their style and comfort, as long as the most important ingredient for the dish is not forgotten – and that is the shrimps. Some people steam the shrimps along with the grains of rice to infuse the flavor more effectively, whilst others cook them separately to be able to control the flavor and texture of the shrimps.

SABZEH POLOW BA MAHI

Preparation time: 2½ to 3 hours
Cooking Time:
Serves: 6
Ingredients

6 white fish fillets
3 cups long-grain rice
3 cups fresh parsley, finely chopped
3 cups fresh cilantro, finely chopped
3 cups fresh dill, finely chopped
20 scallions, finely chopped
1 lemon, juiced
5 tablespoons butter, melted
2 tablespoons vegetable oil
1 teaspoon turmeric powder
4 tablespoons brewed saffron*
salt

Instructions

1. Wash, rinse and soak the rice in salted water for about an hour. Drain the water.
2. In a large pot, heated over a medium flame, bring the slightly salted water to a boil. Add the rice and boil for 6-8 minutes, or until *al dente*. Drain the rice and lightly wash with cold water to stop the cooking process. Set aside.
3. In a large bowl, mix together the parsley, cilantro, dill and scallions with some salt.
4. Evenly grease the bottom of a large pot with 2 tablespoons of melted butter and 1 tablespoon of brewed saffron.
5. Put a layer of the prepared rice in the pot. Layer with some of the herb mixture, and top with another scoop of prepared rice. Keep layering until all the rice and herbs have been used. Ensure the top layer is of rice. Cover and cook over a medium-high flame for 10 minutes.

6.
7. After 10 minutes, uncover the pot and evenly pour the remaining butter and brewed saffron over the rice. Put a towel on top of the pot and cover with its lid. Reduce the heat to extremely low, and cook for another hour.
8. Meanwhile, clean the fish and fry them in a pan with a sprinkle of salt and turmeric, until they turn a golden brown color. Pour lemon juice over them and allow it to be slightly absorbed by the fish before removing the pan from the heat.
9. Arrange the rice on the plate and top it with the fish fillets.

*prepared by steeping a pinch of saffron thread with 6 tablespoons of hot water for 2 hours.

Sabzeh Polow Ba Mahi is a lovely rice fish dish whose name beautifully translates to "Persian Herbed Rice with Fish". Like most rice dishes, the combination of fish with herbs and rice produces a meal that is rich with aroma, texture and flavor – a regal treat for your senses.

Chapter 4

Rice with Vegetables, Grains and Fruits

The agricultural industry of Iran is quite productive which makes fruits and vegetables very abundant. Deemed exotic by most countries, the rich agricultural land and perfect climate makes Iran home to a vast variety of vegetables, grains and fruits. As a top producer of dates, utilization of this sweet fruit in Persian cuisine is inevitable.

Persian Rice Cuisine makes use of all kinds of accompanying ingredients, thus you should not be surprised to find fruits in Persian recipes. More than just a main addition to desserts, Persian Rice with vegetables, grains and fruits welcomes you to flavors you have never tasted before.

CHESHM BOLBOLI POLOW

Preparation time: 1 to 1½ hours
Cooking Time:
Serves: 4-6

Ingredients

1lb ground beef
7½ cups water, divided
2 cups long grain rice
1 cup black eyed peas
½ cup and 1 teaspoon dried dill, divided
1 medium-sized onion, chopped
6 tablespoons oil, divided
2 tablespoons butter
2 teaspoons salt, divided
¼ teaspoon ground black pepper
½ teaspoon turmeric powder

Instructions

1. In a medium-sized pan heated over a high flame, add 4 cups of water and the washed peas. Once boiling, reduce the heat to medium-high and cook for 30 minutes, or until the peas are tender. Drain the water and set aside the peas.
2. In a pan heated over a medium-high flame, sauté the onion with 2 tablespoons of oil for 5 minutes, or until lightly browned.
3. Add the ground beef, black pepper, turmeric powder and ½ teaspoon salt. Sauté for 5 minutes, or until the juices evaporate. Add ½ teaspoon of dried dill and cook for another 3 minutes, or until the meat is fully cooked. Remove from the heat and set aside.
4. In a pot heated over a high flame, add 3½ cups of water, the rice, butter, 3 tablespoons oil and 1½ teaspoons salt. Once boiling, reduce the heat to a medium-high flame and let it simmer, uncovered, for 20 minutes, or until the water is fully absorbed. Remove from the heat, transfer the rice into a container and set aside.
5. Add 1 tablespoon of oil and ½ teaspoon of dried dill to the used pot. Add the prepared rice into the pot and evenly spread it. Sprinkle on top with some more dried dill. Layer the rice with some peas, and top with meat. Continue layering using this pattern until all the ingredients have been used up.
6. Using the handle of a wooden spoon, create several holes in the layered rice to allow the steam to escape. Wrap the opening of the pot with a towel before covering it with its lid to keep the steam from escaping. Let it simmer for 5 minutes on a medium-high heat before cooking on a medium-low heat for 25 minutes, or until a crisp crust bottom has developed. Lightly mix the rice before serving.

In Farsi, the name Chesm Bolboli literally means "nightingale's eyes". Cheshm Bolboli Polow, a.k.a Black Eyed Peas Rice, can also be prepared without the meat to delight vegetarian individuals. As a versatile rice dish, it can also be served with braised beef, chicken fillet, salad or yogurt. And, although this dish might not be visually appealing, you are sure to regret passing the chance to enjoy this delectably tasty dish.

LUBIA POLOW

Preparation time: 1½ hours
Cooking Time:
Serves: 4

Ingredients

1lb beef or lamb, minced
1lb fresh green beans
1 can (14.5oz) tomatoes
4 cups basmati rice
1 cup water
1 medium-sized onion, chopped
2 cloves garlic, chopped
5 tablespoons vegetable oil, divided
4 tablespoons and 1 teaspoon liquid saffron, divided*
4 tablespoons natural yogurt
1 tablespoon butter
1 teaspoon advieh spice mix
1 teaspoon and a pinch of ground cinnamon, divided
1 teaspoon lime powder
salt and ground black pepper

Instructions

1. Wash the rice twice, and soak it in salted water for at least two hours. Drain and set aside.
2. Fry the onions with 1 tablespoon of oil in a pan until golden. Add the minced meat, garlic, salt and pepper, and sauté until brown.
3. Stir in the green beans, tomatoes, ¾ teaspoon advieh, lime powder, cinnamon and 1 cup of water.
4. Allow the mixture to boil, reduce the heat, cover and let it simmer for an additional 30minutes.
5. In another pot, boil the rice with enough salted water until the grains become soft. Remove from the heat, rinse lightly with cold water, and set aside.
6. In a small bowl, whisk together the yogurt and ½ teaspoon brewed saffron. Stir in 3 tablespoons of the prepared rice.
7. In a large pot, heat 4 tablespoons of oil. Add the yogurt mixture. Evenly cover with half of the prepared rice. Top with the green bean mixture, and layer again with the remaining rice. Sprinkle the top with the remaining advieh and a pinch of cinnamon. Drop a tablespoon of butter onto the center.
8. Wrap a towel around the lid and cover the pot. Cook on a high flame for 10 minutes.
9. Pour over the remaining brewed saffron, reduce the heat to low, and cook for another 40 minutes. Remove from the heat and serve warm.

*prepared by steeping a pinch of saffron thread with 6 tablespoons of hot water for 2 hours.

Lubia Polow, popularly known as Persian Rice with Green Beans, is made in such a way that it is a complete meal. The combination of different ingredients makes it a truly one-of-a-kind dish – the sweetness of the cinnamon and the tanginess of the lime blend perfectly. This particular recipe is made with either lamb or beef, making an appetizing dish kids enjoy. Traditionally, Lubia Polow is served plain and matched with any appropriate hot or cold dish.

ZERESHK POLOW

Preparation Time: 4 to 5 hours
Cooking Time:
Serves: 4

Ingredients

1¾ lbs skinless chicken breast
2½ cups basmati or long-grain rice
2 medium-sized onions, grated
4 tablespoons dried zereshk (barberries)
3 tablespoons brewed saffron*
2 tablespoons unsalted butter
1 tablespoon sugar
cooking oil
salt and black pepper

Directions

1. In a dish combine the onions with some salt and pepper. Add the chicken and slightly massage the onions into it. Marinate for 4-5 hours in the refrigerator.
2. Wash the rice twice. Soak the rice in enough water, with 1 tablespoon of salt, for 2-3 hours. Drain the water.
3. In a large pan, add enough water until half-full. Heat over a medium-flame until boiling.
4. Add the drained rice and another tablespoon of salt. Continue cooking for 10 minutes, or until the rice is slightly soft. Whilst cooking, gently scoop the rice from the bottom of the pot and fold it into the surface. Repeat this several times until the rice has become slightly soft. Remove from the heat.
5. Carefully drain the rice and wash it with cold water to stop the cooking process. Transfer to a bowl and set aside.
6. Meanwhile, wash the zereshk with cold water, twice, and drain.
7. In a pan heated over a medium flame, melt the sugar and butter. Mix in the zereshk and cook for 5 minutes.
8. In a small bowl, add 2 ladles of the prepared rice. Add the saffron and mix to coat the rice well. Transfer the yellow-orange rice to the bowl with the rest of the rice. Add the buttered zereshk and toss well.
9. Drizzle some oil onto a preheated grill. Cook the marinated chicken for 10 minutes on each side, or until brown in color. Remove from the heat.
10. Serve the grilled chicken over the zereshk-rice mixture.

*prepared by dissolving ½ teaspoon of powdered saffron with 3 tablespoons of hot water.

Zereshk Polow is also known as Barberry Rice. Barberry is very popular in Persian cooking. Though they are not easy to find anywhere else, most Persian grocery stores will surely have them. Some people prefer to cook the barberries along with the rice when they are being steamed. Doing so would ensure that the color and flavor of the barberries are transferred to the rice.

SHIRIN POLOW

Preparation time: 2 to 3 hours
Cooking Time:
Serves: 4

Ingredients

2½ cups basmati or long-grain rice
2½ cups sugar
1¾ cups boneless chicken
½ cup almonds, thinly sliced and soaked in cold water
½ cup pistachios, thinly sliced
⅓ cup orange peel, thinly sliced
2 medium-sized onions, thinly sliced
2 tablespoons butter
½ teaspoon powdered saffron
Cooking oil
Salt and black pepper

Directions

1. Wash the rice twice. Soak the rice in water with 1 tablespoon of salt for 2-3 hours. Drain and set aside.
2. In a pan heated over a medium flame, sauté the onions in oil until golden.
3. Add the chicken and fry until the chicken is cooked and browned.
4. Add 1 cup of water, salt and pepper. Reduce the heat to low and simmer for 20 minutes, or until the liquid is reduced by half. Remove the chicken and set aside the stock.
5. Reserve 2-3 tablespoons of sugar. Add the rest of the sugar,

with 1 cup of water, into a pot heated over a medium flame. Bring the mixture to a boil.
6. Add the chicken stock, 2-3 tablespoons of oil, and saffron. Mix well.
7. In a pot heated over a medium flame, add the almonds, pistachios and orange peel. Boil for a few minutes and drain well. Repeat boiling and draining twice.
8. Transfer the almonds, pistachios and orange peel to a bowl, pour in some cold water, and let it soak for an hour before draining.
9. Return the almonds, pistachios and orange peel to the pot. Add ½ cup of water and the remaining sugar. Allow to boil for 5-10 minutes. Drain.
10. Half-fill a large pan with water. Allow to boil over a medium flame.
11. Add the drained rice and another tablespoon of salt. Continue cooking for 10 minutes, or until the rice is slightly soft. Whilst cooking, gently scoop the rice from the bottom of the pot and fold it into the surface. Repeat this several times until the rice has become slightly soft. Remove from the heat.

12.
13. In a pan heated over a medium flame, melt the butter with some oil. Add ⅓ of the prepared rice.
14. Spread the chicken over the rice, and layer it with another ⅓ of rice. Add a layer of half of the almond mixture. Top with the remaining rice.
15. Evenly pour the chicken stock mixture over the rice.
16. Cover the pot and cook on a low flame for 30 minutes.
17. Add the remaining almond mixture, and mix well before serving.

This dish is also known as Sweet Rice. Although this particular recipe does not make crispy rice, another version of the Shirin Polow consists of rice with a crispy tahdig, or bottom, for more character. This dish goes well with chicken and turkey, making it perfect for celebrations and special occasions.

KALAM POLOW

Preparation time: 3 to 4 hours
Cooking Time:
Serves: 4

Ingredients

3 cups of basmati or long-grain rice
1lb beef or lamb, minced
1 medium-sized cabbage
1 medium-sized onion, chopped
3 tablespoons brewed saffron*
2 tablespoons lime juice
1 tablespoon tomato paste
1 tablespoon butter
1 tablespoon salt
½ teaspoon turmeric powder
Salt and ground black pepper
Cooking oil

Instructions

1. Tear a few leaves of cabbage and cover the bottom of a large pan. Chop the rest of the cabbage. Set aside.
2. Wash the rice twice. Soak the rice in salted water for 2-3 hours. Drain the water.
3. Half-fill a large pan with water. Allow to boil over a medium flame.
4. Add the drained rice and another tablespoon of salt. Continue cooking for 10 minutes, or until the rice is slightly soft. Whilst cooking, gently scoop the rice from the bottom of the pot and fold it into the surface. Repeat this several times until the rice has become slightly soft. Remove from the heat.
5. In a pan heated over a medium flame, sauté the onions with oil until they are transparent. Add the meat and fry until well browned. Set aside.
6. In another pot, boil a cup of water. Once boiling, add the turmeric powder, lime juice, tomato paste and 2 tablespoons of the brewed saffron. Mix until well combined.
7. Add the cabbage to the pot and cook until soft. Add another cup of water and the onion-meat mixture. Let it simmer until the liquid is reduced by half. Set aside.
8. Add the remaining brewed saffron and 1 tablespoon of oil into the pan lined with cabbage. Add ½ of the prepared rice and spread it evenly. Add a layer of cabbage-meat mixture. Top with the rest of the prepared rice.
9. Using the handle of a wooden spatula, create a few holes through the rice. Spread butter over the top of the rice.
10. Wrap the lid with a towel, cover the pan, and cook on a low heat for 1 hour.

*prepared by dissolving ½ teaspoon of powdered saffron with 3 tablespoons of hot water.

Kalam Polow, Cabbage Rice, is regarded as a very economical way to enjoy a nutritious and delicious dish. This dish is also a good way to introduce vegetables to children. In addition, this particular recipe showcases an amazing tahdig version. This dish is perfect when paired with salads, yogurts and naan (Persian bread).

DAMI BAGHALI

Preparation Time: 3 to 3½ hours
Cooking Time:
Serves: 4

Ingredients

2 cups basmati or long-grain rice
2 cups dried yellow skinless fava beans
2 medium-sized yellow onions, 1 finely diced, 1 sliced thinly
6 tablespoons vegetable oil, divided
2 tablespoons butter
1 teaspoon turmeric powder
½ teaspoon cumin powder
¼ teaspoon red pepper
Salt
Instructions

1. Wash, rinse, and soak the fava beans in 4 cups of water for a few hours. Drain, rinse, and set aside.
2. Rinse the rice before soaking in 3 cups of water, and 2 tablespoons of salt, for an hour. Drain and set aside.
3. In a pot heated over a medium flame, boil the flava beans with 6 cups of water for 30 to 40 minutes, or until slightly tender. During the last 15 minutes of cooking, add ½ teaspoon of salt. Drain the water and set aside.
4. In a large pot heated over a medium flame, sauté the onions with 3 tablespoons of oil until lightly golden brown in color. Add the turmeric powder, red pepper and cumin, and sauté for another 5 minutes.
5. Add the cooked beans to the pot, stir, and cook for a further 5 minutes.
6. Add the drained rice to the pot. Add water so the water level is an inch above the rice and beans. Adjust the heat to medium. Stir in butter.
7. Wrap the lid with a towel, cover the pan, and cook on a low heat for 40-45 minutes.
8. Meanwhile, sauté the onions with the remaining oil on a low flame until they are soft and have caramelized.
9. Serve the rice on a platter and top it with the caramelized onions.

Dami Baghali is also known as Turmeric Rice with Yellow Fava Beans and Caramelized Onions. Just by the translation, you can already imagine it being very tasty. It is best combined with mast-o-khiar, or any kind of salad. This version of the dish is rather simple to make, and is easily customized. It may also be prepared with the addition of tomato paste or meat.

DOLMEH Y KALAM

Preparation time: 2 hours
Cooking Time:
Serves: 4

Ingredients

½lb beef or lamb, minced
1 cup basmati or long-grain rice
½ cup fresh parsley
½ cup fresh tarragon
½ cup fresh dill
¼ cup split yellow peas
1 large white cabbage, cored
1 medium-sized onion, chopped
3 tablespoons cooking oil, divided
2 tablespoons lime juice
2 tablespoons tomato paste
1 teaspoon ground cinnamon
1 teaspoon ground cumin
1 teaspoon salt
½ teaspoon ground black pepper

Instructions

1. Place the cored cabbage into a pot of boiling water. Simmer until the stalks are soft and the leaves peel off themselves. Remove from the heat, drain and set aside.
2. Boil the split yellow peas in 2 cups of salted water until soft.

Drain and set aside.
3. Cook the rice in salted water until it is soft to bite. Drain and set aside.
4. In a pan, heated over a medium-high flame, sauté the onions in oil. Add the meat and cook until well browned. Stir in the tomato paste. Remove from the heat.
5. In a large bowl, combine the rice, meat, peas and chopped herbs. Season with cinnamon, cumin, salt and pepper. Toss gently until well combined. Set aside.
6. Place a spoon of the prepared mixture on the stalky end of a cabbage leaf. Gently roll the leaf and seal by tucking in its sides.
7. In a pan heated over a medium flame, add oil. Arrange smaller, torn and unused pieces of cabbage leaves on the bottom of the pan. Repeat for the remaining leaves, or until all of the ingredients have been used.
8. Arrange the cabbage rolls into the pan, layering them on top of each other.
9. To the pan add 1 cup of water, lime juice and a pinch of salt.
10. Cook on low heat for 1 - 1½ hours. Baste the cabbages with its juices from time to time.
11. Once cooked, carefully remove the cabbage rolls and serve on a platter. Serve with yogurt and salad.

Dolmen y Kalam is a lovely way to enjoy rice, being stuffed inside cabbage leaves. Inside each cabbage package there is a mixture of rice, meat (usually lamb, beef or chicken) and other vegetables. Depending on what you choose, you get to enjoy different textures with every bite. It is a little laborious and very demanding, but the work you devote should bring some fulfillment after each successful attempt. This unique rice dish may be served with salad and yogurt.

MORASAH POLOW

Preparation Time: 2 to 2½ hours
Cooking Time:
Serves: 4

Ingredients

2½ cups basmati or long-grain rice
1¾ cups chicken, skinless and boneless
1 cup zereshk (barberries)
½ cup almonds, thinly sliced
½ cup pistachios, thinly sliced
½ cup raisins
⅓ cup orange peel, thinly sliced
2 medium-sized onions, thinly sliced
3 tablespoons brewed saffron*
2 tablespoons sugar, divided
2 tablespoons butter
cooking oil
salt and ground black pepper

Instructions

1. Wash the rice twice. Soak the rice in salted water for 2-3 hours. Drain the water.
2. Half-fill a large pan with water and boil over a medium flame.
3. Add the drained rice and another tablespoon of salt. Continue cooking for 10 minutes, or until the rice is slightly soft. Whilst cooking gently scoop the rice from the bottom of the pot and fold it into the surface. Repeat this several times until the rice has become slightly soft. Remove from the heat.
4. Lightly rinse with cold water to stop the cooking process. Set aside.
5. In a pan heated over a medium-high flame, fry the onion slices until slightly golden.
6. Add the chicken and cook until browned.
7. Reduce the heat to medium. Add a cup of water, salt and pepper. Let it simmer until the liquid is reduced by half. Remove the chicken and reserve the stock.
8. Wash and rinse the zereshk and raisins with cold water. Fry them separately in oil, adding 1 tablespoon of sugar to the zereshk whilst frying.
9. In a pan heated over a medium-high flame, boil the orange peel in water for a few minutes, then drain.
10. Soak the orange peel in cold water for an hour and drain. Return them to a pot of water with 1 tablespoon of sugar and allow to boil for a couple more minutes, then drain.
11. In a pot heated over a medium flame, add a bit of oil, hot water, and ⅓ of the prepared rice. Evenly layer the chicken on top of the rice. Top with another layer of ⅓ rice. Spread ½ of the prepared almonds, and almond peels, and top with the remaining rice.
12. In a small bowl whisk together the chicken stock, brewed saffron and some oil. Pour it over rice.

13. Reduce the heat to low and cook, covered, for 30 minutes. Add the remaining almonds and orange peel, zereshk, raisins and pistachios. Toss until well combined. Serve warm with butter.

*prepared by dissolving ½ teaspoon of powdered saffron with 3 tablespoons of hot water.

Morasah Polow, the famous Saffron Chicken Rice, is a truly elaborate dish which is usually made for weddings. This dish, also known as the "jeweled rice", combines a handful of ingredients that perks up anyone's taste buds. You can really say that Morasah Polow, amongst the different Persian Rice Dishes, is truly special.

TAHDIG SIBZAMINI

Preparation time: 60 minutes
Cooking Time:
Serves: 4

Ingredients

1 large potato, thinly sliced
4 cups water
2 cups basmati or long-grain rice
½ cup butter
2 tablespoons sunflower oil
2 tablespoons brewed saffron, divided*
1½ teaspoons salt

Instructions

1. In a pot heated over a medium-high heat, boil the rice until it is soft to bite. Drain it and set aside.
2. In a pan heated over a medium heat, combine the butter and 1 tablespoon of the brewed saffron. Add 2-3 tablespoons of water and set aside.
3. In another pot heated over a medium heat, mix the sunflower oil and 1 tablespoon of the brewed saffron.
4. Increase the heat to high, and add the potatoes. Allow to sizzle for a few minutes.
5. Carefully place the prepared rice on top of the potatoes.
6. Using a wooden spoon, carefully push the rice away from the side of the pot to control the crisp texture produced by keeping it at the center of the pan.
7. Evenly pour the prepared butter mixture over the rice.
8. Wrap the lid of the pot with a kitchen towel. Cover the pot and cook on a low heat for 45 minutes to 1 hour.

*prepared by steeping a pinch of saffron thread with 6 tablespoons of hot water for 2 hours.

Tahdig is a Persian Cuisine specialty whose name means "bottom of the pot". This is because it is a special rice cooking method where the rice bottom is crisply cooked. To prepare this dish, it is important that you equip yourself with a heavy bottomed non-stick pan so that you can really cook the rice longer, and make it nice and crisp – a distinguishing characteristic of tahdig.

ESTAMBOLI POLOW

Preparation time: 3 to 4 hours
Cooking Time:
Serves: 4-5

Ingredients

3 cups basmati or long-grain rice
3 cups green beans, cut into 1" long pieces
1 cup brewed saffron*
1 medium-sized onion, diced
1 large potato, diced
1 beefsteak tomato, chopped
1 green chili, chopped
3 tablespoons vegetable oil, divided
2 tablespoons tomato purée
1 tablespoon butter
½ teaspoon turmeric powder
salt and ground black pepper

Instructions
1. Wash the rice twice. Soak the rice in salted water for 2-3 hours. Drain the water.
2. Half-fill a large pan with water. Allow to boil over a medium heat.
3. Add the drained rice and another tablespoon of salt. Continue cooking for 10 minutes, or until the rice is slightly soft. Whilst cooking, gently scoop the rice from the bottom of the pot and fold it into the surface. Repeat this several times until the rice has become slightly soft. Remove from the heat.
4. Lightly rinse with cold water to stop the cooking process. Set aside.
5. In pan heated over a medium heat, fry the onions and potatoes with 2 tablespoons of oil until both appear golden.
6. Add the turmeric powder, tomatoes, chili, green beans and black pepper. Stir and cook for 3 minutes.
7. Add the tomato puree, brewed saffron and some salt. Stir and cook the liquid until it has reduced by half. Set aside.
8. In another pot, add 1 tablespoon of oil. Using half of the rice, make a layer in the pot. Place the green beans mixture on top. Top with the remaining rice.
9. Using the handle of a wooden spoon, create a few holes in the rice. Top with butter.

Wrap the lid of the pot with a kitchen towel. Cover the pot and cook on a low heat for 1 hour. *prepared by steeping ¼ teaspoon saffron thread with 1 cup of hot water for 2 hours.

Estamboli Polow is quite a versatile dish, and is commonly enjoyed by Iranian families in their homes. It can easily be adjusted to fit the diners' preference. This particular recipe does not have any meat, but you can easily combine it with lamb or beef to make a non-vegetarian version. Depending on your liking, you can serve this rice dish with a salad, some kebabs, yogurts, bread or herbs.

RESHTEH POLOW

Preparation Time: 3½ hours
Cooking Time:
Serves: 3

Ingredients

4oz reshteh (noodles), broken into pieces
1 medium-sized onion, chopped
1 cup basmati rice
2tablespoons oil
1 tablespoon butter
salt

Instructions

1. Rinse the rice with water and soak it for 2 hours in salted water before draining.
2. Put water in a large pan and bring to the boil. Add the rice and a teaspoon or two of salt. Simmer over a medium heat until and the rice is soft, but not at all fluffy. Once done, drain, rinse and set aside.
3. In a pan heated over a medium heat, sauté the onions in butter and 3 tablespoons of oil. Add the noodles to the pan and cook until they are golden. Set aside.
4. In a pot heated over a medium heat, add 2 tablespoons of oil. Gradually add a small amount of water to cover the bottom of the pan.
5. Add a layer of rice to the pan. Spread a spoonful of noodles over the rice and top it with another layer of rice. Keep layering until all ingredients have been used.
6. Using the handle of a wooden spoon, create several holes on the rice. Cook on a high heat for 10 minutes.
10. Reduce the heat to low. Wrap the lid of the pot with a kitchen towel. Cover the pot and cook for 1 hour.
7. Serve mixed and warm.

Reshteh Polow is known as Persian Noodle Rice. Although this recipe is rather plain, the dish may be enjoyed with the addition of cinnamon and raisins for a sweet taste. It is a special dish that is mostly served in households the night before Norouz, a famous New Year holiday in Iran.

BAGHALI POLOW

Preparation Time: 1 to 1½ hours
Cooking Time:
Serves: 3

Ingredients

10oz frozen baby lima beans, thawed
3 medium-sized potatoes, thinly sliced
3 cups fresh dill, chopped
1 cup rice
4 tablespoons butter
2 tablespoons brewed saffron*
salt and freshly ground pepper, to taste

Instructions

1. Prepare steamed rice and set it aside.
2. In a saucepan, heated over a medium heat, melt the butter. Arrange a single layer of potato slices on the bottom of the pan. Layer a third of the steamed rice over the potatoes. Season with salt and pepper. Evenly add a layer of half of the lima beans and half of the dill. Top with another layer of steamed rice. Spread the remaining lima beans and dill over the rice, then cover with a final layer of rice.
3. Evenly pour 4 cups of water onto the rice, and top it with butter.
4. Using wax paper, cover the rice. Wrap the lid of the pot with a kitchen towel. Cover the pot and cook over a medium-high heat for 8 minutes.
5. Reduce the heat to low and let is simmer for 35 minutes, or until the rice is soft and fluffy.
6. Setting aside a cup of rice and mound the remaining rice onto the serving plate. Remove the potato slices and arrange them around the rice. Mix the set aside rice with the brewed saffron. Spread the saffron rice over the plain rice.

*prepared by steeping ¼ teaspoon of saffron thread with 3 tablespoons of hot water for 2 hours.

Baghali Polow, popularly known as Lima Bean with Dill Rice, is an exotic Iranian dish that is usually enjoyed with lamb, roast chicken, steak or yogurt. You may opt to add some onions sautéed in butter when you spread the rice, providing more taste and flavor.

ALBALOO POLOW

Preparation time: 3 to 4 hours
Cooking Time:
Serves: 4

Ingredients

½lb sour cherries, deseeded
⅓ cup sugar
2 cups basmati or long-grain rice
2 tablespoons salt
4 tablespoons vegetable oil, divided

Instructions

1. Soak the rice in 4 cups of salted water for 2 hours.
2. Drain the soaked rice. Transfer the rice into another pot filled with water. Bring it to the boil. Lower the heat and let it simmer until the rice is tender. Rinse with cold water to stop the cooking process.
3. Meanwhile, mix the cherries with the sugar in a bowl. Let it sit for 1 hour.
4. Transfer the cherries into a pan, heated over a low heat, and let it simmer for 30 minutes. Remove the cherries and reserve the cherry juice.
5. In a large pot heated over a medium heat, warm the oil. Transfer half of the produced cherry juice into the pot. Spread half of the prepared rice on the bottom of the pan. Cover with the cherries and top with the remaining rice.
6. Mix the rest of the cherry juice with 2 tablespoons of oil. Evenly pour it over the rice.
7. Wrap the lid of the pot with a kitchen towel. Cover the pot and cook over a medium heat for 20 minutes.
8. Remove the kitchen towel. Mix the rice mixture. Cover and cook for another 5-10 minutes.

Albaloo Polow is also known as "Sour Cherry Rice". Sour Cherry, *Prunus cerasus*, is also known as wild cherry, and it is native to Europe and Southwest Asia. It is a fruit that is more acidic than sweet, but gives off a very characteristic flavor .This makes sour cherry a good ingredient to be used in the preparation of various dishes. On its own, sour cherries are good in resolving sleep problems due to its melatonin content, but in this particular rice dish, it brings a perfect taste and color to a very enjoyable meal.

Chapter 5

Saffron in Rice

Rice or "berenj" was believed to have been brought to Iran from an Indian subcontinent thousands of years ago. The variety of rice opens Persian cooking to an adventure when it comes to rice cooking. In addition, being a staple ingredient to most Iranian meals, a lot of chefs have come to find ways to enhance the dining experience of their guests through the use of rice.

As already mentioned in the first few chapters, Persian Rice Dishes are prepared in several ways. In this book, however, we categorized them into three main methods: Kateh, Polow and Dami. One ingredient not mentioned in the opening chapters, but ever present in the recipes, is saffron. Saffron plays a very important role in Persian cuisine, especially in the cooking of rice, and this chapter will briefly comment on this special ingredient.

Saffron (Zah'Fa'ron), *Crocus sativus*, is an exotic and valuable ingredient. It is the most expensive spice in the world; one pound of which is derived from the stigma of about 70,000 to 250,000 purple saffron crocus flowers. Manufacturers of the spice hand-pick the flowers in the autumn when they are in full bloom, just so they can be brought to kitchens all over the world to provide some color, taste and aroma to various dishes.

The use of saffron has been referenced back to ancient Rome and Egypt, where it was used as a dye, as a drug or as a perfume component. It wasn't initially popular as an ingredient for culinary pursuits, but it has grown, and is continually growing in popularity and usefulness. It became commercially in demand in Iran and Spain (the most reputable producers), as well as in Morocco, Kashmir, Egypt and Turkey.

More Facts about Saffron

- Probably the most important thing you need to know about saffron is that you must keep the usage at moderate levels. Saffron in large doses can cause sleepiness that can lead to convulsive laughter, and may cause fatalities.
- Iran produces about 96% of the world's supply of saffron. Their production is known to be the highest in quality.
- The aroma and flavor that saffron produces is truly unique and cannot be duplicated through artificial means.
- Saffron is available in two forms: powder or threads. These two forms are used differently in the kitchen. Threads are more complicated because they need to be steeped; powder saffron is simpler to use and is fairly straightforward.

The use of saffron in cooking is as much of a science, as well as an art form. To take advantage of the true flavor saffron brings to your cooking, you have to know how to manipulate it so that it releases the right amount of flavor and aroma. In other words, it demands true culinary talent and skill to properly utilize it.

The Saffron Plant

As already mentioned, saffron comes from the saffron plant, *Crocus sativus.* The stigma, the female part of the plant, is removed from the flower. It is then dried, or cured, and sold commercially. This flower grows abundantly in Iran, as well as in Greece, Spain, and India. It blooms in the autumn with a single plant producing several flowers during the season. Each flower usually produces three stigmas, and each stigma contains the distinguished saffron flavor, dye and aroma.

Chapter 6

Summary

Basically, you are now heavily equipped and prepared to do some basic Persian Rice cooking. Cooking is an art, and Persian cooking, like most of the oldest cuisines of this world, follows a deep science that may never be found anywhere else. More than the perfect taste and experience, when you follow this route, you are embracing ancient Iranian culture and tradition, along with all the health benefits their dishes provide.

Persian cooking is all about balance – the dishes exhibit perfect balance that is not only good in fulfilling your desires to satisfy your palate, but also with your aspirations to building a strong mind and body. The foods in most Persian menus are made from ingredients that are meant to revive the body. Most Persian foods combine a variety of ingredients like fruits, poultry, herbs, petals, blossoms and seeds. One impressive fact about Persian cooking is that many of the ingredients used are components incorporated into the manufacture of medicines. Like in the ancient times, food has been important for the maintenance of health, and this is what you will benefit from when you choose to go Persian.

Another important thing for you to note is the difference between home cooking and restaurant dining. The Iranians regard home cooking so much more special because the labor devoted to every dish prepared at home is given more thought, more heart and more care. It is for this reason that when catering services are hired, clients expect the food to be of the same level as a home cooked meal, and nothing less. As a home cooker, therefore, you must understand that a lot is being expected of you. Nevertheless, let the pressure inspire you rather than scare you from trying. Exploring the culinary world of Persian cuisine is going to be an adventure – a dip into the ancient world of Iran where flavor and taste are truly divine.

www.ingramcontent.com/pod-product-compliance
Lightning Source LLC
LaVergne TN
LVHW020427070526
838199LV00004B/312